ILL-ADVISED RECOMMENDATIC
FOR THIS BOOK

D1553675

"Kyle Flak is like Doc Brown from *Back to the Future* because he actually believes that by arranging all of his holy junk and ugly love into the right shape and allowing lightning to strike he can create the magic that will one day heal his heart. In other words, if you cut this book open, a rabbit will fall out."

~ Ben Kopel, author of *Victory*

"Kyle Flak's poems are like dispatches from a distant but familiar planet. As much mournful as hopeful, as much nostalgia as there is joy. I loved this book."

~ Jensen Beach, author of *Swallowed by the Cold*

"Finally, a writer who has no idea what poetry is."

~ Mark Leidner, author of *Beauty was the Case that They Gave Me*

"I wish that Kyle Flak would just get a real job, move out of his mama's basement, and never write a single word ever again."

~ Kyle Flak's high school guidance counselor

I AM SORRY FOR EVERYTHING IN THE WHOLE ENTIRE UNIVERSE

I AM SORRY FOR EVERYTHING IN THE WHOLE ENTIRE UNIVERSE

KYLE FLAK POEMS

Gold Wake

for Alfred E. Neuman
for Leo Fender
for James Tate
for muh Mama and muh Papa
for Leslie Haberkern
for Steve Maesen
for The Grand Rapids Public Library
for pastrami
for Lake Superior
for Bob Barker
for Del Shannon
for the many Earls of Sandwich

THINGS

"Then I went back into the house and wrote, It is midnight. The rain is beating on the windows. It was not midnight. It was not raining."

~ Samuel Beckett

POLITE INTRODUCTION BY KYLE FLAK'S SECRET GHOST WRITER, KYLE FLAK

I don't know if this thing actually matters.

I am not even a smart guy or anything.

I don't know anything about trees or mathematics.

You might be better off just going on a road trip

with your friends

where you laugh

and

eat super buttery toast

at one of those beautiful old timey diners

that make you feel like

you are the special someone

who has just become

the new Garrison Keillor,

but then you talk

and, no, your voice is still your own,

so, no, you did not actually

just turn into Garrison Keillor;

you are only at an awesome diner

as a fresh cool alternative to

actually reading Kyle Flak's new book

and who the hell is Kyle Flak anyway,

some kind of descendent of Polish meat market owners

who has earned a living from packaging toothbrushes

at some point during his life?

Yes.

You're exactly right.

That is exactly who he is.

And I have to admit

that even to write this stupid introduction thing

is actually very hard work for me.

I have to admit

that even to get an "F" on Larry Bergman's eighth grade

science homework was very hard work for me.

4

So, I'm sorry if this book

turns out to be really terrible

and can't fix the toilet in your summer home, grandma.

I'm sorry that I am just a regular guy

who wrote this for fun one weekend

when there were no *Hanging with Mister Cooper* reruns on.

It seems like pretty much everyone I know

from school

wishes that they could just be Pa Ingalls

from *Little House on the Prairie*

without all the hard work, pain, and suffering

because, yeah, he was so cool!

But as for me, I am just Kyle Flak.

I love sandwiches, cartoons, and long walks alone

in various dark and creepy abandoned warehouse

type of buildings.

Oh, yeah, and also:

please buy lots of copies of this ordinary book to share

with your wonderful friends and

family members!

I swear that it is a unique document,

just like *Choose Your Own Adventure* book #112,

Skateboard Champion,

which was my favorite book for all of grade school

at Immaculate Heart of Mary Catholic School.

My second favorite book was *A Few Minutes*

with Andy Rooney by Andy Rooney.

I wrote "Clem Smith" in the dust jacket of

my copy because I wanted my name to be Clem Smith.

Speaking strictly as an uninvolved third party,

my poems might be valuable to someone

someday because they might

save the human race

from everything

that threatens humanity,

even if they are

just completely terrible.

A poem only says, "I have feelings. Please remember

that everybody else has feelings, too. The end."

I know that this poem is not perfect, but neither

is Wade Boggs, and he is still cool.

Also, here, one wants to thank Anthony Guerriero

for being a really nice person who used to give new middle names

to everyone.

Also, here, one wants to mention that I wish I had written

a three hundred page

introduction to put on a zero page book.

I also wish that Piers Anthony mostly wrote

"author notes."

I also wish that Stephen King mostly wrote "On Writing" books.

My favorite animal is the moose.

My favorite color is called "sonic blue"

or maybe actually I like the one called "Daphne

blue" better, but I can't really remember

so let's just say that I like 1950's shades of blue—

the kind of blues

that look like May skies before May proms

in small Midwestern towns where everybody's

nice and mostly just wants to rake leaves for grandma,

and it doesn't even matter which grandma

they rake leaves for

cause they've always got a rake in their

car ready to go

and every grandma they pass in their car

will always be kind enough

to alert them if there are ever any leaves around

that need to be raked up.

Yup.

That's the kind of blue I mean.

So, now we can begin.

We haven't really begun yet.

This is just an introduction or something.

I have probably already failed or something.

But who cares?

I am only one man.

And I have already broken

most of the things that I know how to break.

THE STRANGE AND UNFORTUNATE CASE OF MISTER SPRINKLES

"How did you know that she was the right one for you?"
I asked my teddy bear, Mister Sprinkles, who had just
Married my pet cat, now called Misses Sprinkles.

Then I made my teddy bear growl as he said, "She just
Drives me crazy and I love it! I love it when she drives me crazy!"

Then Mister Sprinkles wailed on a tiny toy saxophone
Like he was the happiest guy on Earth,
And I was really just about getting ready
To believe that, when suddenly something else
Happened that I won't bother to mention
Until much later in this poem, or possibly never.

I mean, he has such a wonderful coat of fur,
And also such a kind, decent, loving
Retro Las Vegas
Kind of heart space!

Tonight he will be performing as Guy Sprinkles
With his new band called The Sparkling Sprinkle Ponies.

They do mostly 50's rock and roll hits
For old ladies to dance to.

But none of the old ladies ever bother to show up.

The performances take place
On my kitchen counter
Right around midnight.

I have to say,
That I'm honestly not doing so bad these days.

Honest, it's true.

I am only thirty-three years old,
I have not died of bronchitis,
My beautiful mother writes me the most wonderful Christmas
letters right around Easter time, plus I am nearly recently
        divorced from everyone
And only constantly in a state of complete and utter
        unemployability / financial disaster.

My new money making scheme is just to hold on tight
And silently prepare myself for a really big crash.

I feel pretty lucky most of the time.

For instance, my toothbrush from middle school
Is still not completely worn out yet.

The bristles may look like a banana slug
That someone really horrible has just recently stepped on,
But I swear I can probably still get
Maybe three or four more years out of the thing.

Also, today a really cute young girl asked me out on a date,

So I ran far far away
Until I was high atop the Mulick Park sledding hill,
Where she would probably never even think
To go looking for me
Because I really am
Almost as old and decrepit

11

As I always so insistently
Say that I am.

Sometimes I wonder if anything anyone ever says about me is
    actually true,
Like: "He thinks the Alamo is a person
Who grants free wishes to children?"
Or: "He wants to smell like a wet unbathed llama
On the hottest day The Texas Zoo has ever known or dreamed
    of."

Life is pretty hard.

That's why I'm standing here in my family room without any
    family around.

That's why I talk all day long to a delightful old teddy bear who
    has more verve, spunk, moxie, and gumption than the
    whole starting lineup for the 1957 Brooklyn Dodgers.

I don't even know what gumption means and here I am using the
    word gumption.

This is a good sign.

This is a good time to sigh.

One time I fell asleep for a whole entire year
And then someone else wrote this with my typewriter
And also put my name on it.

I don't know what this is.

"I hope it is a belated birthday present for me, Mister Sprinkles!"
Says Mister Sprinkles

All ready to go
With an awesome kick ass birthday hat on his head
And a jug full of an artificially flavored green drink
Called "artificially flavored green drink."

Seriously, that's all it says on the label.
We bought it from a man who was also selling snakes
Out on the mean streets of Akron, Ohio—
A city famous for its fishing tackle, mud wrestling, dirigibles, and
        waffle cones.

At night I walk around aimlessly,
Praying for delicious and nutritious random stalks of broccoli
To fall down from the sky
To save all the little people from starvation
And pain and sadness and madness, etc.

There really is no cure for anything, is there?

Not even love.

Why, even now Misses Sprinkles is tearing the nose off of
        Mister Sprinkles' face with her claws.

How terrible.

How awful.

"How great!" say delighted TV audiences everywhere,
Swiftly handing me
My token briefcase full of unmarked hundreds
To spend on boob jobs and exotic foreign cars.

And then I laugh and laugh

13

Until my whole stinkin' head falls right off.

It rolls up a hill and then down a hill.

Where it stops,

No one knows.

PERSONAL HISTORY

I was born
Southern and broke
Inside a toothpick factory
With bleeding gums
And a passion for Neil Diamond music

My mother was a cast iron skillet
Used mainly
To rattle my skull
During times of
Great stress

We had no car

We had to ride tiny toy donkeys everywhere

Oh how the other children
Would laugh at us
As we made our way to school
With only a single jar
Of expired pickled eggs
To share
Between the ten of us

Let me see
There was: Jim Bob, Ray Bob, Bo Bob, Sally Bob, Carrie Bob, Susie
Bob, Aaron Bob, Joaquin Bob, Harry Bob
And me—Bob Bob.

And we were all curly haired, red eyed
Rhino nosed losers

Working in coal mines after school
Just to try and stay afloat
In a cruel and oppressive world
Where all known or suspected daydreamers
Were punished for every single daydream
They were either known to have had
Or were suspected to have had

Our monthly daydream bill
Amounted to
Approximately
$897,650,791.01!

So we were always in trouble with the law,
Always running away from the town sheriff
Who owned dozens of fake moustaches
And each one he wore
Was more capable of disguising him
Than the previous one he wore

He was almost impossible to detect!

Except that he was the only one in town
Who wore fake moustaches

So actually
We always saw him coming

Nobody could know what he would do to us
If he ever actually caught us

But we imagined many horrific possibilities

"Now take off your clothes and sing the theme song from the hit
     TV show *Cheers*"

"Now eat these tiny red hot candies until you get moderately
        tired of eating these tiny red hot candies"

All in all
Life was pretty good

We knew our place in the world

And the yellow sun
Bloomed high in the sky
About once every
Five decades or so

As we all grew old

Gnawing on pine cones, rolling around in dusty piles
Of other people's abandoned bandages

Waiting for the haunting sound of the loon
To wake us up each morning

A loon sound we grew more and more in love with everyday

But it came from a loon we never saw
And never got a chance to talk to

So it could have just been a simple audio recording
Played on a hidden tape recorder
Buried beneath the op-ed page
Of the weekly coupon cutter junk mail newsletter type of thing
We usually slept on

Out on the mean cold streets
Of Bangor, Maine

Which really is actually a southern city

If you would only look north
For once in your life

All the way north to Halifax

Dear sweet gorgeous Halifax—

A city
Surely made

Entirely out of gold!

DULUTH VS. PITTSBURGH!

The loudest thing I've ever heard is a dinosaur screaming at me in one of my dreams. It said, "Do not go to Pittsburgh." Whoa, man! My ears are still ringing. But, nonetheless, here I am, still in Pittsburgh!

In some ways, it's a fine city. For example, we have a guy here who handcrafts wooden unicycles out of trees he raised himself!

But, of course, I still do miss Duluth. If Duluth were a woman, she'd be Jane Seymour's character in *Dr. Quinn Medicine Woman*, Dr. Quinn Medicine Woman.

Sometimes I get up really early, before even the birds are awake and just moan and wail, thinking about Duluth. I've got a "Twelve Months of North Country Fun!" calendar that features Duluth on both the January page and on the August page, but really that is not really enough Duluth for me. Enough Duluth for me would pretty much be if I basically just became Duluth and got to feel each part of myself in well, yeah, I guess pretty much a rather sexual way, I don't know.

Anywho, so my ex-wife Lucy called me up the other day and said, "Look, I know we've had our share of differences, but maybe we could just meet up again, here in Duluth, and kind of sort of just see how things go?"

What? Where did that come from? Wasn't she the one who, like, threw a hot ham biscuit at my head and didn't even care that there was tasty expensive real Dijon mustard gradually seeping into my already really pretty irritated eyeballs? I was like, "Honey, baby, you know I got seasonal allergies and my eyes also get irritable and reddish anyway because I don't sleep too doggone much, now why'd you go and throw that hot ham sandwich at my face?"

Her only explanation: "Whoops. Forgot about the Dijon."

Forgot about the fucking Dijon??? What the fuck?

I don't understand people. I don't understand people who don't pay attention to their mustards.

First you got your classic yellow, then you got your spicy brown, then you got your fucking Dijon. It's like way up there, see where I'm pointing? Way up at the sky. I'm talkin' way up there. Higher than birds go. Like fucking outer space and shit. Dijon spends time with dead saints and shit. Up there above the clouds, playing harps, napping when everybody else gotta go to work and shit down here in Pittsburgh.

So, like, fuck, as much as I love Duluth—is home really a place where loved ones pretend that Dijon mustard just, basically, doesn't exist? Like it's some vapory phantom that dwelleth only in the crazed imaginations of coked up disco dreamers and barely legal mad scientists with the idea of tenure taken to its full maximum selfish advantage and shit? A place where the phrase "warming zesty Parisian sting" doth have no meaning, no effect, no weight, no gravity, no political power or freedom???

Yeah, I'm gonna call that Lucy back, tell her her presence totally ruins the pristine natural beauty of the great city of Duluth. Its hills, its waterways, its shoreline, its eateries, it charming little side streets—all ruined while she's still in town.

THE SEXY MYSTERY PARTY

1.

The thing about sexy mystery parties is that you can never predict exactly when one is going to happen.

You might be driving your car on some strange mountain road that you never really ever drive on, but then all of the sudden you notice that "Hey, this isn't even my car!" And then you look down at your elegant cashmere scarf and also likewise say something like "Hey this isn't even my elegant cashmere scarf!"

There will be other people at the sexy mystery party. How foolish it would be to have a sexy mystery party all by yourself!

Don will be there.

Already you can see him smoking his fancy imported cigarettes with his fancy imported cigarette holder.

And you will most definitely want to say to him when you see him, "Don, why you gotta be so fancy all the time?"

And Don, this Don guy he'll respond with a series of astonishing facts.

"The cobra has no legs but the donkey has four of them."

"My wife is employed at the Marquette County Dairy Queen."

"When writing in cursive it is best to know what you are doing."

Damn you, Don, for being such a beautiful personage.

2.

"When the dog smiles at me and the fake waterfall in the lobby smiles at me and the living room couch smiles at me, I say it is high time that I had myself another slice of your gorgeous pineapple upside down cake, Madame Brunwald."

We were all having a pretty good time.

Jenny, she was the one who leaned towards me near the grandfather clock to say something no doubt very beautiful and enlightening and mysterious and so forth but just as she did so the grandfather clock erupted with all of its various chimes and whistles and bird squeaks and panda screams so that I could not hear the very beautiful and enlightening and mysterious and so forth thing that our dear guest Jenny was trying so hard to communicate to me via her small and perfect voice.

And then she slowly walked away.

And I noticed how the back of her dress—it didn't exist at all!

"I am going to walk toward the room where the shower is. And I am going to do it very slowly and very nakedly. So, you had better watch the way that all of my very fresh and very healthy skin moves. It will move as if heaven and hell are so close to each other that one of them must surely soon go out of business embarrassingly and therefore meaningfully, if these are actually words, words in English, words in English that mean something..."

That was my first impression of Jenny.

3.

Later on, we discovered a way to drink martinis while also drinking some martinis.

The cops showed up in order to do the same thing. The same thing that we were all doing.

Jenny, I think, had discovered a room where no one else realized that a room could even exist.

She was very busy there becoming more beautiful and also preparing to show everyone where the room was.

4.

The year was probably 1923 or 1924 and everyone in the whole world was interested in sexy mystery parties.

A sexy mystery party must contain a few naked people.

A sexy mystery party must contain at least two big burly men with mighty big handlebar mustaches who agree to hold a long and tiresome boxing match out on the front lawn.

A sexy mystery party must contain some very exotic and very dangerous household pets. Like: a crocodile, a panther, or an elephant.

A sexy mystery party must not end until at least a week after it begins.

A sexy mystery party must contain no fewer than 100 guests.

A sexy mystery party must contain at least one billionaire and one Nobel Prize winner.

A sexy mystery party must contain vodka and gin and seltzer and limes and no other beverage except black coffee.

A sexy mystery party must have nonstop live music by many excellent and famous musicians who no one has ever heard of.

A sexy mystery party must be held in a house that is very old and very large.

That is all.

Thank you.

NICK ADAMS MY ASS

Reading Ernest Hemingway

I always feel a little bit terrible

About not becoming as awesome as he was

He used to grab a fish right out of the lake, bite down on it, then
pour some whiskey in his ear, make love to a
washerwoman in a washing tub, travel to Buenos Aires by
hot air balloon, drive some scrambled eggs down a dead
war hero's throat,

And then sit down in the woods

And write 10,000 beautiful hungry sentences

Before dawn

Even kissed his moustache

A moustache

Made entirely

Out of

Songshine

HELLO

"Hello" is Bryant Gumbel's favorite word, but sometimes he says, "cello" instead of "hello" to throw people off; it is his little way of getting revenge on a world that has never thrown him the most awesome pontoon boat party in the universe—no, that award, the award for "most awesome pontoon boat party in the universe" obviously went to Brian May from Queen, who once threw a pontoon boat party that lasted for thirty seven years back in the late 1970's; time was very different back then; nobody knew what the hell was happening, but there was Brian May with his nonstop pontoon boat party that everyone loved and adored; Prince Valiant, the famous character from the most boring comic strip ever invented was there for the full thirty seven years of it—"No regrets, dudes, just tryin' to live my life and stuff," he said during a recent telephone interview conducted for this one short piece of exciting microfiction/prose poetry/who the fuck can tell what it is so what's the fucking difference that was first honestly conceived in the sparkling parking lot of a modern disco supply store where Rod Stewart was happily buying a three liter bottle of rose petal daydreams for his illegitimate son, Bryant Gumbel, who was already getting mighty fidgety in the car after having endured a lifetime of undue criticism for basically just trying to be a regular and decent "good enough" sort of guy, the kind of guy we all aspire to be, in our dreamiest of dreams, the kind of dreams that Brian May just grabs and grabs with his greasy agile hands until they can become just one long shitfuck of an awesome guitar solo.

I LOVE THAT ONE POEM
BY RAYMOND CARVER

I love that one poem by Raymond Carver where he

writes about wanting to wake up really early

one more time

sometimes I imagine that I am a famous writer smoking a
            cigarette

while I type on a typewriter

in a little rented room

above a bakery

I imagine that I survive

on what I find inside the bakery's dumpster

and also the bakery

gives me this attic room

because I sweep up the floor of the bakery every night

after I am done

working on my novel about

a young man who is secretly

in love

with

a cute innocent neighbor girl

who also happens to be

the mayor's daughter!

also

the young man's father

is the leader of

a secret organization

that is actively trying to

completely humiliate

and eventually destroy

the mayor!!!!

mornings are like this:

I pace around

oddly

imagining that my life is really free

that there is no one who is truly suffering

that everyone's floating on a cloud

that my boss at work doesn't actually hate me

that flossing isn't actually important

that being a shoe horn collector

is actually

a really smart and cool new hobby to have

the lights in this city

start turning on

at approximately 7 a.m.

so that means that if you wake up around 3 a.m.

you get

about four good hours

of being "off stage"—

no drama is occurring

no actors are acting

no enemies are busy planting

conflicts

for you

to barely resolve

later in the day

when you are tired

from waking up so early

to enjoy this—

ah, this!

the silent sound of no one thinking

the silent sound of a house that ain't getttin' no action

the silent sound of nobody correcting anybody's grammar or
        posture or anything

but now

it is almost 9 a.m.

and I am already

no longer really safe!

pretty soon, people will look in my window and decide that I'm

somehow

ruining America by believing in imagination and happiness and
feelings and people and joy

Bernadette Mayer once wrote in one of her poems something
about how certain writers used to be called "candle
wasters"

I don't know if that's true

but if it is

I always want to be a candle waster

because I am a human fucking being

not a robot

and everybody's got stuff to say

that only a blank page

would ever

bother

to listen to

CARNIVORE DOLLS

After tuba practice, I went to the mall to look at Carnivore Dolls. I've got: The Bobcat, The Crab Eating Mongoose, The Eurasian Badger, The Ethiopian Wolf, and The Giant Panda. I ain't got: The Bush Dog, The Aardwolf, The Spotted Hyena, and multiple various others. My Dad only lets me get one at a time, which is totally lame. Johnny Bronson just gets the whole damn Annual Set mailed to him year after year after year—the lucky bastard. One of these days, I'm just going to run away from home, become my own Carnivore Doll, eat whatever stuff gets in my way. Mailbox: chew, chew, chew. Ice Cream Truck: chew, chew, chew. Homework: chew, chew, chew.

Yeah. Chewing's good. But now I've got to decide what I'm going to tell that crummy old man who sits behind the counter. The one who really controls my fate. The one who can either let me or not let me play with the European Pine Marten right in the store. That thing is fucking great. He's feisty. He's moody. He's grouchy.

He eats rodents, birds, and beetles. Also: he's an excellent tree climber. Whenever I get to play with him, I make him climb all over the fucking place. He gets on people's sweaters. He gets on people's heads. He taunts and flaunts. He coasts and boasts. His fur is brown and full and lush. You really wouldn't want to get on his bad side because even his good side is basically a bad side.

Yup. He's one rough dude.

I really hope that I will get to play with him today. Play with him for own particular purposes.

Which basically are: to harm. To harm and to harm and to harm.

PERFECT YELLOW DRESS

This night was made for your perfect yellow dress

I stand around
Talking to random dudes and laughing and stuff
But really

This night was made for your perfect yellow dress

I look at it and look at it

We will never be this young again

The full moon will never be this big and strange
And haunting again

This backyard will never contain
So many happy tipsy people again

This midnight grass
Will never know so many soft and splendid footsteps
Again

Clearly,

This night was made for your perfect yellow dress

I watch it as it easily absorbs
The many bright enchanting flavors of our
Humble little
Eastern Kentucky
Version of springtime

I watch it as it says hello to caterpillars, owls, ants, and
        maybe also a few sleepy dreamy newborn baby tree
        squirrels

I watch as it quietly notices that it is so much better than cake,
        so much better than sex,
So much better than a fresh cheap gallon
Of our very own
Sweet sweet
Cherry orchard wine

This night was made for your perfect yellow dress

Everybody seems to notice it
Everybody seems to want to dance with it
Everybody seems to want to play with it
Everybody seems to want to try it on
And eventually "have their way with it"

Everybody seems to be completely and utterly unable to
Healthily resolve
Their own severely overexcited
Complex emotional state
About it right now

And also it is almost the merry jolly month of May

So it is almost a really good time
To drive around aimlessly
In a shiny new convertible
Until you fully discover
That there is a secret lemon scented seashore

Hiding inside your very own cocky crooked creepy
Wholly forgiven good enough for anybody
But also way too cool for school
Lilac coated heart space—

And so, yes, surely, of course, I really do believe

This night was made for your perfect yellow dress

With its many startling new age disco prophecies
With its many shocking unearthly erotic enigmas
With its ego and its pomp
Its diamond gifting implications
And romantic vacation inspirations

With its obvious reminder of death
And its completely untamable desire to taunt and torture us all
Forever and ever amen—

Yes,

This night was made for your perfect yellow dress

A night wide open and full of endless echoing promises
That trail the stars
And emit billowy sighs
Inside a poof of
Mossy
Friendly
Gradually escaping
Vapory
Yellow tree mist

That we will always notice and remember

Whenever anything slightly interesting happens

Or also

Whenever anybody ever opens their mouth
To scream,

"Aha!"

MONDAY

Fun Monday. Super fun Monday. Ice cream cone Monday. BOGO Monday. Life of the stars Monday. Leaping lizards Monday. I just bought the leaning tower of Pisa Monday. Listening to Van Halen records until we puke Monday. Riding bikes and playing tag Monday. Something in my shorts is scratching my ass for me Monday. Baseball cards and tequila in the summer sunshine Monday. Buying shoes online and paying for them with a stupid new credit card I hate to use Monday. Cole slaw Monday. Firefly Monday. *Hanging with Mister Cooper* rerun marathon Monday. Rubbing my coworker's friggin' aching to high heaven lower back Monday. Stroking it and toking it in the basement without her sweet love Monday. Hi I just joined the gym but am waiting for the right day to actually go there Monday. Popcorn & *Jaws* on VHS Monday. Swimming in my best friend's pool while he works on some information technology homework in the kitchen with his wife named Delores Monday. Buying a karate outfit for my kid who will probably hate karate Monday. The ocean is beautiful and I just want to touch it but I can't cause I got jury duty and a headache from hell Monday. Fun Monday. Super fun Monday. Ice cream cone Monday. Play in the hay Monday. Rollerskatin' all the way to the afterlife Monday. Sunshine & glossy meadows Monday. Tambourines & baked goods sales Monday. PBS pledge drive & cute new piglet salt shakers from a yard sale down the road Monday. Hooray for my IRA & my reliable brand of denture cream Monday. Baked salmon & apricot sherbet Monday. Crab cakes & sweaty drippy makeup Monday. She walked into the room like an orchestra pit looking for its lead tuba and was surprised to find me with my pants already down Monday. The loons are singing softly down by the marsh where somebody's grandpa died last year by puma attack Monday. It's the sale of the year and I'm on the sofa I already know I love and care for and all that crap Monday. This is a poem and you're damn right it could just go on forever for no reason at all kind of Monday. Your hair's a mess but everybody loves your apple pie and tiny tooter kind of Monday. Let's celebrate America and smoke a lot of grass kind of Monday. I've been typing for hours with a really bad hangover Monday. Nobody ever reads the obituaries in my town anymore because everybody's already dead Monday. My ex girlfriend is a bank robber and a hooker and a cheating exhibitionist who loves caramel delight Girl Scout cookies kind of a Monday. Oh, Monday, we love you! But also: please just go away from us and die already.

HOW ABOUT WHAT

"I should be watching really great movies with my sunglasses
on," I say out loud to my cat.

"Meow meow," says my cat

But really she means "Please do go on."

Also: "Please type me a beautiful new sentence about a fish."

And so I type, "Sometimes I forget that whales even exist."

And then she glares at me hard, like

"Whales are not fish, they're mammals like me. I can't believe you
actually own me."

Then she purrs like a llama on mescaline

Exciting all the hairs on my fuzzy old man cactus

As a bunch of fragrant rainbows

Instantly burst

Then electrify

The Houston night sky

And suddenly for, like, half a second my life is not boring at all,
even to sex addicts.

Then my wife tells me to mow the lawn

And I'm all like, "No, I'm busy being happy"

Which is a lie

Cause already I'm worried about the next sentence

About what it could mean to various people, like the people of
New Hampshire

For instance

Who are so often ignored

That no one would ever really bother to puke in rage about their
lives

Their tiny little New Hampshire lives

Fireplaces & apple cider

Polite jogging & maybe once in awhile a slightly amusing

Little bow tie or something.

"I'm sorry

I just want everybody to be in love with the sound of

A toothbrush

Falling into a toilet bowl" I say to my wife,

Cause

That is what this poem is really about

In case you were wondering

It is what all my poems are really about

I am always thinking of that moment

It happened once on a TV show called *Seinfeld*

Jerry dropped his lady's toothbrush in the toilet and he didn't tell
    her

So then he couldn't kiss her without thinking about toilets

It was a very big problem

He almost lost his mind over it

I can't remember how it got resolved

Maybe he just "liked" something on Facebook

Or rode an antique prairie schooner all the way to Sante Fe!

I really don't know

Actually I am writing this after surviving a pretty busy day of
    work where I sent faxes for

People and

Talked to cute girls about their reading habits

So I am really very tired

But I hope that we can still be friends anyway

That is what is important to me

I want you to invite me over for

Lemon bars some time

Right in the cool

Of a crisp autumn evening

When you were just up late listening to Yanni music anyway and
needed

"A hand in the kitchen"

Someone to stir things up a bit

Someone to be around

And chat about nothing

Until whenever

I have always dreamed about something like that—

A nice friendly group of little lemon bar buddies!

And you seem pretty cool

So hey

How about it?

I WANT EXACTLY NOTHING

F. Scott Fitzgerald was eating a double decker ham and salami sandwich inside a 2016 Ford Fusion. His double deckers were basically just where he bought two ordinary ham subs at the deli and then stuck them together and started eating them. He had come back to life in the late 1990's to go to a Smashing Pumpkins concert, and then just kind of stuck around, laying low, taking it easy.

Of course he still had some unresolved issues with life. He wondered vaguely about a sort of weird in between kind of zone he had frequently operated in but never totally figured out or fully understood. It was a zone where a person was experiencing enormous desire, enormous difficulty, and enormous tranquility all at the same time. He liked to call it the "green zone." If he had ever been a soccer coach he would have told his players, "You folks all stayin' in the green zone? Well, whatever—you should. Okay, now on to wind sprints..."

"It is a little known fact that F. Scott Fitzgerald would have made an excellent soccer coach," F. Scott Fitzgerald said quietly to himself. He thought about all the young champs he could have made, all the little squirts he could have taught the virtues of discipline, self reliance, and perseverance to. "I could have saved 10,000 souls if I had only been a middle school soccer coach," he said.

He never believed that any of his books had done much of anything for anybody. He hated the way that so many people mistakenly thought his message was "be as rich as possible and as drunk as possible," when really his message was "forgive me father for I have sinned greatly."

The autumn leaves were gorgeous, so Fitzgerald revved up the engine on his modern, sensible sedan and took a little drive out to Reeds Lake in East Grand Rapids, Michigan where the famous *American Pie* screenwriter had grown up. In the afterlife, Fitzgerald had become a huge fan of Eugene Levy's role as Jim's father in the film. Eugene's performance presented fatherhood as something where "to everything there is a season." In Eugene's performance there is both shrewdness and kindness; respect and disdain; harmony and discord; understanding and disapproval; friendship and isolation; discipline and play. For a long time, Fitzgerald was basically just waiting for Levy to die so that he could hang out with him on a yacht he had rented from Saint Judas, but then he got tired of waiting around and also heard about the alternative rock movement and also wanted to dye his hair a strange color, so yeah.

The lake was shockingly blue today, a new fresh wet blue, the kind of blue you could just live in forever. Fitzgerald got out of his car and walked around, right up close to the lake. It was a gorgeous day, almost as gorgeous as heaven except that here there were problems. That guy over there has a cold. The woman in short shorts tonight will gain Chlamydia but lose her virginity. The fella walking the dog wants to stab a broccoli crown into his neighbor's ear hole. Life is strange; death is so easy, yet both offer so many true and valuable insights for the aspiring novelist. "You should totally do both" would be F. Scott Fitzgerald's general advice to anyone questioning the value of either realm.

Taking in the bright warmth of the day, Fitzgerald soon found that he was starting to crave an ice cream cone and that he was also starting to feel a tremendous sense of gratification from refusing to give himself one. The sunny was so sunny; it was like God was calling him on the telephone, wanting to ask him if he could just bring back an Eddie Murphy comedy video from Blockbuster, but wait there were no video stores in this town anymore so why didn't God know that? Maybe it was just a test; maybe all this complexity and struggle in the land of the living was just a test. "No," Fitzgerald told himself, "It is both a test and not a test. Life is Whitmanic. It is large and contains multitudes. Saint Augustine was one of the world's greatest sinners and so he became a clergyman and began documenting the details of his wrongdoing, hoping that in the documenting he could gradually become a good seed of sorts."

And now, more in the zone than ever, Fitzgerald started thinking, "Hmmm. Maybe mint chocolate chip or maybe butter pecan or maybe both or maybe an extra large serving of a kind I really hate, like lime sherbet."

This was totally "it", the thing Fitzgerald had been waiting for all his life and all his death. He liked the shock value of desiring something so stupid after leading such a grand majestic existence.

Obviously, he was reminded of Orson Welles in *Citizen Kane*, except he felt that his own situation was somehow superior because ice cream shops aren't as corny and childish as sleds are.

"Ice cream shops are way damn serious, like volcanoes are serious, like baseball games are serious," he found himself saying out loud to the stranger in front of him in line. It was a little girl, who simply ignored him.

He imagined Kane's last words as "fudge ripple sundae with cherry sauce" and got a strange thrill. Revising movie scripts was no crime. Every good thing can and should easily turn into another good thing. And it was really pretty great to think that he could basically just think and decide forever about this stupid ice cream cone situation and then just show up at the register to say the line he'd been waiting to use in real life since about 1941 or thereabouts: "Ring me up, you filthy ragamuffin. I want exactly nothing."

UNGRATEFUL DWEEB

Then there was that one time when I saw the 1990's grunge
      rocker J. Mascis buying some

Lunch

Downtown.

I wanted to tell him

Something.

"Your guitar sounds like what I was really going through
      whenever I walked by

That one girl's house in high school

When I was shy and scared and hoping she'd

Suddenly

Come right out of her house

Completely naked

Holding a large pizza and a two liter bottle

Of my favorite soda."

But instead I just thought really quietly

"There he is. My old high school hero.

He actually exists and actually buys lunch sometimes."

This was all in Amherst, Massachusetts

A town so mild and polite

That it really did need a 1990's grunge rocker living in it

For everybody to feel okay

For everybody to not fall asleep at 7:30 pm before

Jeopardy even came on.

I guess there was also Emily Dickinson's house and grave,

But the songs by J. Mascis' band Dinosaur Jr.

Really seem to contain Emily Dickinson's ghost

So my theory is

That she is just always haunting J. Mascis' guitar or something.

So a song like "In a Jar" is really a case of

"One stop shopping" as far as moderately wild things

To ever come out of

The town of Amherst, Massachusetts are concerned.

And also

As an interesting side note

I think that teen angst never really goes away

It just takes on new forms, like,

The old man

Who sullenly feeds the ducks at the graveyard

While getting really angry at his own pair of Velcro shoes!

"All my buddies still wear lace ups. How did I get to

Be so old," he says to his only true best friend,

Commander Wigglesworth, a fourteen-year-old

Canadian mallard with five children and a bright yellow beak

That kind of says, "Howdy world, my head is green and I
        loooooove

Stale bread crumbs that have been torn up and thrown at me

By seedy old men and delightful little children with weird flavors

Stuck to their hands that more often than not

Wind up

Affecting the flavor of my

Daily bread doses."

But then

Also what the heck was I doing

Just skulking around

Marquette, Michigan five years ago wishing that I could

Suddenly become

The largest lake sturgeon

To ever live in Lake Superior???

Oh, I guess I was just mourning my missing past,

Like Jay Gatsby's life warned us not to do.

But it's so much fun that one can almost never not do it
        constantly—

All those wonderful moments that I can so plainly see now

That I missed or didn't miss but failed to take more advantage of
        more fully!

Oh, those moments!

A two liter of gross syrupy soda will do nothing at all

To bring you back!

But still I walk around near all my "sacred places" hoping that

"Okay, now it is sixteen years ago again. You can

Take the cool senior to prom in your fragrant jalopy. You can

Remember to do 1,000 push ups every morning so your

Arms will look awesome forever, you can win the

State mathlete competition, you can go bowling all night

Without saying a single dumb thing, you can study really hard

And become a mad but not totally evil scientist who invents a
   cure

For every major disease and thus rewins the affection of all

The nice people who ever chose to hate you, you can stare at
   the stars,

Buy a pet doggy, eat a bunch of tacos, write a bestseller, win a
   Grammy,

Wrestle a tiger, stock up on stock in Google, meet the President,

Go to the state fair, be a decent lovable fellow, get your acne
   cleared up,

Play an integral role in world peace by refraining from even

Throwing a single snowball at anybody ever again, et cetera, et
   cetera, et cetera

Amen."

The possibilities are endless

Just like today or

Any day, really

For which

I am probably

Always a little bit

Completely ungrateful.

HOUSEPLANT

Alvin was one of those people who had always wondered what it'd be like to spend time with other people. But mostly, he just hung out with his houseplants. One of them was actually enrolled in several online university courses. Alvin encouraged the houseplant in her studies. The studies were basically fictional. The houseplant had no discipline. The houseplant had no stamina. The houseplant had no drive. Sometimes Alvin wanted to put the houseplant in jail! But that wouldn't do. Alvin was a lonely boy who often dined for years on the same one exact kind of soup. The current flavor was: lime potato goat blush. It was pinkish and didn't have an actual ingredients list on the package, which might be illegal. Alvin bought his food at garage sales. The cans could be from anywhere. The cans could contain anything. He was brave in this way. Sometimes he sat all alone on the sofa with a huge set of elk antlers on his head, praying. It was very important to pray. Alvin's life was not in order. He thought outer space looked kind of orderly. If only he could see his own life from about 10,000 light years away! Then everything would be clear. Then everything would be easy. Then he wouldn't have to be so sad all the time. Then he wouldn't have to be engaged to marry a houseplant that didn't have any goals, any ambition, or at least a reasonable respectable amount of income from some random stupid job or real legitimate type of investment deally thing.

HOW TO HAVE A FUN WEEKEND!

1. Buy the most expensive pair of boating shoes you can find, then slice 'em, dice 'em, and serve them up in a hearty Bolognese sauce.

2. Leak weird green fluids directly from your bowtie.

3. Start assigning specific seats to total strangers right in the middle of a really great movie at a really great movie theatre.

4. Cry loudly into a microphone during the long boring bus ride from Pittsburgh to Duluth.

5. Sign up for free guitar lessons, then call 'em back to quit. Sign up again, then call 'em back to quit again. Repeat as needed.

6. Stare at a punching bag for hours. Try to punch its lights out with your eyes.

7. Memorize the lyrics to "Blank Space" by Taylor Swift, then never use those lyrics for anything ever for the rest of your life.

8. Slowly ponder death.

9. Learn how to draw a robot!

10. Square dance the hell out of somebody's else's $250,000 fancy wedding on Cape Cod.

11. What is time? Write a full length poetry book manuscript about time in strict iambic pentameter using only the first ten letters of the alphabet.

12. Take a rowboat out to the middle of the ocean. Then: drop the oars into the ocean. Can you make it back to work before Monday morning????? If you do make it back, show up wet and frantic at your boss' desk and make sure several fish fall out of your sweater vest and onto his Important Work Related Documents.

13. Watch *Weekend at Bernie's* first thing in the morning and then try to figure out where the hell you can go from there.

14. Someone is knocking at your door. Use your awesome ninja skills to climb out the bathroom window, sneak up behind them with a lawn mower, and say, "Thanks for mowing the lawn! You did an awesome job! Here's twelve bucks!" Then turn into a worm and quickly vanish into the depths of the earth for the remainder of your existence.

15. Learn how to read Mozart sheet music like it's just easy instructions for how to prepare microwavable macaroni and cheese.

16. Visit and evaluate a wide variety of nearby waiting rooms.

17. Do the same thing with weight rooms.

18. Compare and contrast: waiting rooms vs. weight rooms.

19. Spend all weekend seeming despondent and hopeless while actually feeling lighthearted and snappy.

20. Buy an ice cream cone. Instantly drop it. Say, "Uh Oh!" in a really slow, loud, obnoxious way. Weep pathetically on an isolated bench where a few curious people can observe you nervously without ever getting involved.

BOLOGNA SANDWICH

I want to eat a bologna sandwich with you,

Long lost love from another era

And another location

This is really a big moment for me

To suddenly decide like this

I was just picking my nose in an aviary

And then I thought

"Hey, what's the trouble with my loins?"

And then that famous silver sparkle

I sometimes feel

At the bijou

Started tickling me

I want to eat a bologna sandwich with you

Long lost love from another era

And another location

The stars all awesome in the sky

The Lake Superior waves crashing down on our one cute puppy
     who is definitely very excellent at swimming and will
     probably be okay out there for a little while longer at least

I want to eat a bologna sandwich with you

Long lost love from another era

And another location

With fancy imported mustard

Mustard imported from Apollo, the god of music/poetry/ light/
     whatever

His hand reached down and gave it to us

"Here, here you go. Here's some delicious mustard

For yer tasty sammiches"

A pack of chocolate covered raisins also in my pocket

Ready for whenever

I want to eat a bologna sandwich with you

Long lost love from another era

And another location

Memories from all the dorkiest moments of our lives drifting
    swiftly through our heads

Your obsession with Knute Rockne's knuckles, my obsession
    with collecting oil rags from famous auto repair
    specialists

Your obsession with buying Swedish surf rock records and then
    translating all the lyrics arduously into Cantonese, my
    obsession with being really sad all the time and imagining
    that "help I'm trapped inside the world's tiniest tube of
    artificial leather glove ointment"

I want to eat a bologna sandwich with you

Long lost love from another era

And another location

The bees buzzing in an open field

As your sullen pink blouse drops down

61

And you too

Become an open field

And my body

It is a tractor

A noisy disgusting chugging tractor

Rolling over potholes and sludge

Traveling from over a million miles away, probably from outer
     space somehow

Traveling like it's worth all the spacebucks in the universe

Just to catch a glimpse

Of your

Charming

Vintage face

BILL GROMROOTH'S DAD

On Saturday nights, I like to take my baby down to the diner

So that we can consume many chocolate malts

In the good kind company of our fellow

Stevesburg Central High School fighting walruses.

My buddy Ed just always orders the "endless plate o'

Catfish nuggets" and boy oh boy

Can that guy

Sure make sure

To always get his fill.

He almost pushes the limit

Of what is morally acceptable

To ask a restaurant to do

For the price of one third of an

Average sixteen-year-old's

Normal middle class allowance.

And speaking of money,

One thing that I would really like to do

In the near future

If it is frankly at all possible

Is just

Basically

Win a whole bunch of free money

From some weird and

Unexpected source

Like maybe a karate tournament

Or a really exciting

Radio call in contest.

I mean,

My AGI, or

"adjusted gross income"

As reported on my

Federal "1040 a" tax form

Was way below

What it normally costs to be a really interesting and fun big deal

In this town.

Like, for instance, Bill Gromrooth's dad,

Who owns not only his own vinegar business

But also his own mustard business

And his own ketchup business—

The guy's loaded!

He drives around town in a truck that looks like a pleasure palace
        on wheels—

A really sweet ride

It must have cost him more than a few pretty pennies from hell

Just to

Even dream about getting

A thing like that.

But hey

Look at me

I've got my pretty baby

And right now she's wearing a bright yellow skirt that almost
        seems to reinvent the whole

Idea of bright yellow skirts!

But I guess

Actually it's really more orange

Now that I bend over to look at it again

This town is so dusty

It's hard to see anything clearly, see anything as it really truly is.

But, still

It doesn't take a Don Diego De La Vega

With the secret identity of "Zorro" or

As the Americans like to call him "the Spanish word for fox"

To figure out that life is still pretty exciting for everybody
nonetheless

What with our chocolate malts and stuff

And football season just around the corner

As it always is

And always should be.

NINE TINY ESSAYS ABOUT TREES

1.
Electric guitars are made out of trees. And other stuff. I feel sad when I think about a cool dude up on stage waving a dead tree around.

2.
Once, I took a walk in the woods. And all I heard was the sound of my dead lover taking off her baby blue sweater, waiting for me to come touch her.

3.
I was at the museum with my uncle and I told him, "I love breezes in treezes." He looked at me like I was a poisonous snake trying to sell broken stereo equipment to children.

4.
"Not all trees can sing and dance and make love to beautiful strangers—but I can!" said the tree in my dream who looked a lot like Michael Bolton.

5.
Deep in winter, I walk to work on icy sidewalks. And the trees hold out their tired arms to welcome me.

6.
Any slob can get a job, but only trees can stand really still in the autumn rain like they are the mighty gods who have always owned the sound of loneliness.

7.
I played the Mozart piano sonata perfectly. Then I looked out at the rain and noticed that the trees were playing a song that made the entire collected works of Mozart suddenly burst into flames and vanish from the face of the Earth.

8.
"Tea anyone?" I say to the empty hallway, then laugh out loud. Of course I am alone. My favorite people are trees.

9.
For a long time, I wrote nothing. Then my arms woke up by themselves and created a bunch of strange documents that I honestly know nothing about. I have always been asleep. Asleep and dreaming of trees.

I AM SORRY FOR EVERYTHING
IN THE WHOLE ENTIRE UNIVERSE

I am sorry for loving beauty.

I am sorry for being so horny.

I am sorry for being interested in beer, liquor, coffee, candy, poker, and flowers.

I am sorry that I have never won a tennis match.

I am sorry that I never pay attention during board games.

("Dude it's your turn again." "What?")

I am sorry for having a low grade point average.

I am sorry for wanting to spend all night walking around alone instead of going to the place where your birthday party is / was.

I am sorry for loving people in very awkward and silly kinds of ways.

I am sorry for hating rules, obligations, chores, multitasking, authority, and discipline.

I am sorry for taking so many sad lonely bus rides to strange towns for no particular reason or purpose.

I am sorry for wasting the best years of my life by just getting drunk and in trouble with a bunch of my foolish and rowdy friends.

LAST WORDS

I like buying giant jars of mayonnaise

And then just letting them sit in my basement for ten or thirty
years.

These foggy days

Make me think about just

How pleasurable it is to do that.

Oh, sigh.

Will the rain ever come really soon to wash away all my terrible
sins?

Some people accuse me of being too passionate about

Talking in a really loud voice all the time

So that the neighbors can hear my exact opinions about various

Unlikable game show contestants.

To them I say: fie, fie, fie!

I am proud to have a hairy back.

I am proud to not be a lanced sore.

Love is like this:

You used to be a really annoying used car salesman dressed in an
    ugly plaid sport coat

And now you still are.

ACKNOWLEDGMENTS

Thank you to Ma, Pa, Crall Schmall, Davey, Cheryl, AJ, Miles, Eli, Lily, Tracy, Laura, Nathan, Grandma, Natalie Jackson, Chris Grabiel, Geik Geiken, all other folks in the Flak / Lawrence realm, etc.

Thank you to the whole Amherst / Northampton / Belchertown crowd: James Tate (1943-2015), Dara Wier, Peter Gizzi, Stanley Crawford, James Haug, David Bartone, Zach Savich, Jeff Downey, Hilary Plum, Jensen Beach, Anne Holmes, Mark Leidner, Ben Kopel, Jack Christian, Miranda Dennis, Kimberly Abruzzo, Caroline Cabrera, Gale Marie Thompson, Nathaniel Otting, Mike Young, Rachel B. Glaser, Francesca Chabrier, Lily Ladewig, Sara Boyer, Rachel Katz, Matthew Suss, Mike Wall, Jono Tosch, Kristen Evans, Adam Parker Cogbill, Phillip Muller, Carlin Mackie, Sylvia Snape, David Fleming, Amherst Books, Amherst Typewriter and Computer, Amherst College, The Jones Library, The Belchertown Library, McCarthy's / Cathay's, and that one guy at the ginger ale store on Main street who always said "You again!" angrily whenever I went there to buy ginger ale.

Thank you to Ronald Johnson, Austin Hummell, Beverly Matherne, Russell Thorburn, Dianne Sautter, Jennifer A. Howard, Rebecca Johns Trissler, Bryan with a Y, Matt Hudson, Dan Welling, Randy Tryan, Leslie Haberkern, Dan Kane, Johnny "T Slide," Phil Molnar, Amanda Frederick, Eric Benac, C.R. Dobson / D. R. Frogson, Richard Monroe, Adriaan Ostrander, Ben Cline, Alex Pontois, Casey Thayer, and all the other bold brave Upper Peninsula people from my Marquette days.

Thank you to Mark Schutz, Matthew Francis Kemp, Scott Kemp, Ryan Farley, and anyone else who ever hung out with us during high school even though we were dorks.

Thank you to the super fun senior Art I class table: Mike, Bernadette, Amanda, etc.

Thank you to Dan Stauffer, Matt Iacopelli, Jacob Caya, Alex Povilus, John Paul Bida, and the rest of the IHM 1990's crew.

Thank you to Steve Maesen, Steve Assarian, Steve Tompkins, Steve Maxim, and other Steves I know from the library.

Thank you to Christina Aderholdt, Jeanne Clemo, Kyra Vanhorn, and Victor Puhy from GRPL-GO.

Thank you to Julie Beukema, Karen Thoms, Nic Coppernol, Elaine Bosch, and all the other wonderful GRPL people I have known and enjoyed over the years.

Thank you to Jim Kacian from The Haiku Foundation.

Thank you to Michael Sikkema, Jen Tynes, W. Todd Kaneko, Amorak Huey, L.S. Klatt, and other Grand Rapids poetry people who have been super nice and super fun.

Thank you to Kyle McCord and Nick Courtright from Gold Wake Press for their kindness, patience, generosity, and encouragement.

Thank you to LK James for her awesome artwork.

Thank you to all of my previous editors for teaching me so much, especially Adam Robinson, Gary Metras, Tim Staley, and Jeremy Hanson-Finger.

Thank you to *Cacti Fur, Dragnet, Jokes Review, Soundings East,* and any other magazines / websites / anthologies where some of the writings in this book first appeared.

Thank you to various other celebrities, writers, and heroes etc. who have oddly served as role models for me over the years: J. Mascis, Conan O'Brien, Rod Serling, Jimmy Stewart, F. Scott Fitzgerald, Dan Sklar, Basho, Walt Whitman, Larry David, and muh Papa.

Thank you to everyone else I accidentally forgot to put on this list.

Also: I am sorry if I accidentally got anyone's name wrong. I did the best I could.

FREE SECRET BONUS MATERIAL!

GREAT CLASSIC SANDWICHES FOR YOU TO TRY AT HOME!

1. THE KYLE FLAK SANDWICH: Karate chop one whole grain rye hoagie roll in half. Fill hoagie with butter, popcorn, and a bunch of old sad memories from The War. Eat it in front of the TV on a TV tray with the TV on. Mostly just watch the commercials and weep.
2. LAZY DAY SANDWICH: Fry two fluffy buttermilk pancakes in elk's blood. Surround result in camouflaged hope and various laundromat fantasies where the new girl in town actually wants to take a look at the frightened quail trapped inside your cupola.
3. TOUGH GUY SANDWICH: Hang around town for a bit, then maybe get in your car for a while. Maybe something you heard on a radio at some point was kind of like a sandwich. I don't know.
4. LOSER SANDWICH: Poke holes in a random soft pretzel. Call your Mom from the beautiful shiny phone at the beautiful shiny neighbor lady's house. Tell her about the way the tomato crop looks from where you're standing. Tell her that your life is not really a complete sandwich. It's just little odd random bits, the kind of stuff that most people would just probably say to throw away.

CLOSING THOUGHTS: DOES THIS BOOK HAVE ANY HISTORICAL SIGNIFICANCE?

*~ A Brief Afterword
by Amateur Historian Bryan M. Reickert, M.A.*

In short, this book has no historical significance whatsoever. If I had to describe its place in history with a single word it would be "forgotten." Mr. Flak is not William Shakespeare, Emily Dickinson, or Walt Whitman. I mention these few exalted names only to highlight how few poets are actually remembered by anyone. Can we truly expect a book of poetry written by an unknown hipster/stoner/sluggish layabout to have any real greater significance? The answer is no. Definitely no. I can confidently say that this book and its author are sure to remain safely unknown for a great many years to come.

ABOUT GOLD WAKE PRESS

Gold Wake Press, an independent publisher, is curated by Nick Courtright and Kyle McCord. All Gold Wake titles are available at amazon.com, barnesandnoble.com, and via order from your local bookstore. Learn more at goldwake.com.

Available Titles:

Kelly Magee's *The Neighborhood*
Keith Montesano's *Housefire Elegies*
David Wojciechowski's *Dreams I Never Told You & Letters I Never Sent*
Mary Quade's *Local Extinctions*
Adam Crittenden's *Blood Eagle*
Joshua Butts' *New to the Lost Coast*
Mary Buchinger Bodwell's *Aerialist*
Becca J. R. Lachman's *Other Acreage*
Lesley Jenike's *Holy Island*
Tasha Cotter's *Some Churches*
Nick Courtright's *Let There Be Light*
Kyle McCord's *You Are Indeed an Elk, But This is Not the Forest You Were Born to Graze*
Hannah Stephenson's *In the Kettle, the Shriek*
Kathleen Rooney's *Robinson Alone*
Erin Elizabeth Smith's *The Naming of Strays*

ABOUT KYLE FLAK

Kyle Flak was born in Grand Rapids, Michigan in 1983. His previous things of poetry include: *What Hank Said on the Bus* (Publishing Genius, 2013) (Winner of the Chris Toll Prize), *The Secret Admirer* (Adastra Press, 2010), and *Harmonica Days* (New Sins Press, 2009). In 2013 he was a finalist for a Ruth Lilly Poetry Fellowship from The Poetry Foundation. In 2015, he was chosen as a "Poet to Notice" by Grandma Moses Press. His writing has appeared in numerous magazines and anthologies. He studied at the MFA Program for Poets and Writers at the University of Massachusetts at Amherst.

CPSIA information can be obtained
at www.ICGtesting.com
Printed in the USA
FFOW02n1934040417
34129FF